Facing Africa

The African Art Collection of The Toledo Museum of Art

Mary Nooter Roberts

Toledo, Ohio
1998

in memoriam Kurt T. Luckner

This book was published with the assistance of the Andrew W. Mellon Foundation.

FIRST EDITION

ISBN 0-935172-07-6
Printed in the United States of America. All rights reserved under International and Pan-American Copyright Conventions.

Acknowledgments

It has been a great pleasure to work on this exciting project with the staff of The Toledo Museum of Art: Sandra E. Knudsen, who has overseen every detail of this book from conception to completion, and whose encouragement and vision have been inspirational; David W. Steadman, Director; Nadine Smith and her dedicated and insightful advisory committee; Nan Plummer; Christine Mack; Rochelle Slosser; and many others who have contributed to this project. I am also grateful to many distinguished colleagues who have generously shared their expertise and/or field photographs. They include: Monni Adams, David Binkley, Barbara Blackmun, Herbert M. Cole, Joseph Cornet, Eberhard Fischer, Anita Glaze, Lorenz Homberger, Alisa LaGamma, Frederick Lamp, Babatunde Lawal, Joseph Nevadomsky, Nancy Ingram Nooter, John Pemberton III, Allen F. Roberts, Doran H. Ross, Vicki Rovine, A. Turconi, and Susan M. Vogel. While I am grateful for the assistance of all these friends, I alone am responsible for the content of this book. I dedicate this book to my husband, Al; our children, Sidney, Seth and Avery; and our parents, Nancy and Robert Nooter.

Mary Nooter Roberts

The Toledo Museum of Art
2445 Monroe Street
P.O. Box 1013
Toledo, Ohio 43697-1013
Telephone (419) 255-8000
Fax (419) 255-5638

Project Supervisor: Sandra E. Knudsen
Toledo Museum Photographs: Tim Thayer, Oak Park, Michigan, and Photography, Inc., Toledo, Ohio
Field Photographs: As cited in the captions.
Editor: Sandra E. Knudsen
Designer: Rochelle Slosser

Map design by Lorenzo Walker from the book *African Art: Virginia Museum of Fine Arts,* by Richard B. Woodward. © 1994 Virginia Museum of Fine Arts, Richmond.

Composition: Emigre Arbitrary Bold and Adobe Garamond.
Printed on Allegra Gloss Text by University Lithoprinters, Inc., Ann Arbor, Michigan.

Front and Back Covers: *Yoruba Epa Helmet Mask, attributed to Bamgbose or Areogun, 1977.22 (see page 9).*

Title Page: *Detail, Luguru High-Backed Stool, 1994.21 (see page 45).*

Contents

Africa

This map shows the name and approximate locations of each culture represented in this book along with the boundaries of Africa nations as they exist today.

Mediterranean Sea

MOROCCO
TUNISIA
WESTERN
SAHARA
ALGERIA
LIBYA
EGYPT
Red
Sea

S A H A R A   D E S E R T

MAURITANIA
MALI
NIGER
CHAD
SUDAN
DJIBOUTI

SENEGAL
GAMBIA
Bamana
BURKINA FASO
NIGERIA
ETHIOPIA
SOMALIA
GUINEA-
BISSAU
GUINEA
Senufo
GHANA
Yoruba
Benue River
Bangwa
CENTRAL AFRICAN
REPUBLIC
Temne
SIERRA LEONE
Dan
Guro
Edo
Yaure
Owo
Baule
Akan
LIBERIA
TOGO
CAMEROON
IVORY COAST
REPUBLIC OF BENIN
Fang
CONGO
Mangbetu
UGANDA
KENYA
EQUATORIAL GUINEA
GABON
Kota
DEMOCRATIC
REPUBLIC OF
CONGO
RWANDA
BURUNDI

Niger River
Nile River
Congo River

ATLANTIC
OCEAN

Kuba
Songye
Luba
TANZANIA
Luguru
INDIAN
OCEAN

ANGOLA
ZAMBIA
MALAWI
MADAGASCAR

ZIMBABWE
MOZAMBIQUE

NAMIBIA
BOTSWANA

SWAZILAND
SOUTH AFRICA
LESOTHO

Preface

The Toledo Museum of Art has a small but choice collection of the art of sub-Saharan Africa. Collecting began forty years ago, in 1958, with the acquisition of the Benin Queen Mother head (p. 17) and the Fang Ngontang mask (p. 59). Works of African art were collected seriously by a few individuals and museums in Europe and the Americas starting only in the late nineteenth century. The earliest collections, like that of the Detroit Institute of Arts begun in the 1890s, were assembled largely because of curiosity about exotic cultures. In the early and middle years of the twentieth century, avant-garde artists such as Pablo Picasso, Maurice Vlaminck (who owned the Fang mask), Amedeo Modigliani, and Constantin Brancusi were intensely influenced by the expressive power of sub-Saharan and other non-Western art. Today, we are also deeply interested in understanding the cultural traditions and aesthetic heritages of Africa and of the people of African descent in the "melting pot" of North, Central, and South America. Works like these by African artists provide a memorable way to see their cultures, representing the faces, social contexts, and perceptions of other avenues of human life.

New accessions made it possible in 1973 for the Toledo Museum to open a gallery devoted to the art of Africa. Works of art, all of the highest quality, continued to be acquired under the guidance of Kurt T. Luckner, curator of ancient art, until his untimely death in 1995. With the exception of the ivory Owo figure (p. 19), which dates from the sixteenth or seventeenth century, most of Toledo's objects were made in the nineteenth or twentieth centuries. The sometimes harsh effects of a tropical climate have caused the loss of many earlier works of African art in wood.

For many years Toledo visitors have requested an up-to-date, popular book about our African art collection. The fall 1998 exhibition "Soul of Africa: African Art from the Han Coray Collection" provided the impetus to publish. We are grateful to Mary Nooter Roberts for a stimulating manuscript and for her on-going counsel as we reinterpret and reinstall our African art. We are also thankful to the community advisory group that worked to define the goals of the book that became *Facing Africa* and to assess its design and text: Deborah Carlisle, David Guip, Linda Nieman, Kim Penn, Shirley Sebree, and Nadine Smith. They encouraged us to try to focus on the needs of families with children and of educators whose students want to understand other cultures, as well as those of gallery visitors. We owe a special debt to Mrs. Carlisle's fifth-grade class at Fall-Meyer Elementary School for several lively workshops that ruthlessly evaluated how the Museum displays, interprets, and teaches African art and culture. We hope the readers of this book will enjoy the process of "facing" Africa—"turning toward," "confronting," and "connecting with" the art and people of Africa—as much as we have.

David W. Steadman, *Director*

Facing Africa

It is your head that you have to worship....
Your head is more important than anything.
Your head is what you should pray to.
Anytime you want to pray ... take a kola nut
and put it on the forehead, not the chest ....
One's head is more important than any part
of the body.... It is the controller of the body
... it is destiny.

(Yoruba saying)[1]

This book presents the many faces of Africa through a celebration of The Toledo Museum of Art's African art collection. The masks and figures, pendants and dolls, shrine figures and altarpieces, of the Toledo Museum's collection depict faces, heads, and both human and animal features that forge bridges between ourselves and the world. The faces in this book are those of mothers, children, heroes, queens, noblemen, spirits, and animals. Through an analysis of their exquisite forms and multifaceted functions, this book teaches about African art and culture while also teaching about ourselves. The faces of these works are depictions of universal human concerns, such as birth, education, entertainment, governance, prestige, power, and death. As we face the works in this collection, we face Africa across the Atlantic; and in that mirror we find eloquent reflections of a shared humanity.

Faces and heads are central to African artistic expression. Some ethnic groups in Africa have complex philosophies pertaining to the immense importance of the head and the life force that it contains. Luba peoples in central Africa define the head as the seat of wisdom, power, and intellect; and in spirit possession

rites the spirit comes to "mount" the head of a diviner, offering him or her enlightened vision and divine insight.[2] Among Yoruba peoples of Nigeria, all people are thought to have both an "inner head" and an "outer head." The inner head is the seat of intentions, perceptions, and intuitive knowledge, and the locus of a person's essential nature (*iwa*), while the outer head is the vehicle for the outwardly expressive nature. A Yoruba proverb states, "May my inner head not spoil my outer one."[3]

Shrines, where works of art are kept, are the faces of divinity or the "faces of worship." They are "places of meeting, of facing the gods and locating oneself relative to the cosmos."[4] Similarly, masks are threshold devices that form bridges between ourselves and others, between past and future, between nature and culture, and finally, between this world and the other. The diverse faces and figures in this collection-sculpted from wood and ivory, cast in brass and gold, laden with copper and beads-attest to the masterful ways that African artists express the deepest dialectics of human experience. Together, the inner and outer aspects of these works impart life-enhancing values to those who behold them.

When a Luba diviner of the Democratic Republic of Congo takes possession of a spirit, she dons a beaded headdress called nkaka to contain the spirit in her head. Nkaka is the name for a pangolin, a scaly anteater in Africa whose tough, overlapping scales are impervious to predators even as fierce as leopards. Once possessed, the diviner uses her enhanced powers of perception and clairvoyance to determine the cause of a client's misfortune and to prescribe a remedy. Photo: Mary Nooter Roberts, 1989.

Facing Page: *Orangun-Ila, a Yoruba king, wearing his great beaded crown which symbolizes the spiritual "inner head" of the king and links him with his royal ancestors, who have joined the pantheon of gods. The inside of the crown has been consecrated with secret medicinal herbs to augment the king's ase, or life force. The occasion is the Odun Oro, the festival for the king. Photo: John Pemberton III, 1984.*

Epa Helmet Mask: Mother of Twins (*Iyabeji*)

Yoruba Peoples, Nigeria

Attributed to Bamgbose (Osi Ilorin, Opin, Ekiti region, d. 1920) or Areogun (Osi Ilorin, Opin, Ekiti region, ca. 1880–1954)

Mid 19th to early 20th century

Wood, pigment; H. 49 1/2 in. (125.7 cm), Weight 24 lbs. (10.9 kg)

Purchased with funds from the Libbey Endowment, Gift of Edward Drummond Libbey, 1977.22

The Mother of All

The face facilitates communion with the
supernatural.... For what has a "face" is
accessible.[5]

African artists give a face to the invisible
forces of the universe and to the tenuous
but sacred links that bind humans to one
another and to more inaccessible realms. This
virtuoso sculpture has been attributed by
scholars to two artists of different generations.
While it was once thought to be the work of
Areogun, the openness of this mask's design is
more characteristic of Areogun's teacher of
sixteen years, master sculptor Bamgbose, who
died in 1920.[6] Often, a master executed the
principal stages of a work and delegated
completion to his assistants. It is possible that
this mask is a work by more than one hand.

Among Yoruba peoples, artists are highly
valued not only as master craftsmen but also as
ritual specialists. They are remembered and
honored through eloquent poems called *oriki*
that praise particular qualities and contribu-
tions of the individual sculptor:

> He carves hard wood as though he were
> carving a soft calabash....

> The expert, whose sculptures dazzle the
> beholder....

> One who knows how to carve appropri-
> ately for kings. (Praise song for Areogun)[7]

The importance of the head and face as
metaphors for a community are explicit in this
monumental mask. It possesses the many faces
of mothers, children, men, and women in a
composition that emphasizes hierarchy,
support, and interdependence. The central
image of a mother of twins alludes to extraordinary fertility, longevity, and the interrelation-
ships of nurturing and sheltering, supporting

and sustaining, that perpetuate and promise
societal growth and continuity. Below the
composition is another face shaped like a pot—
a somber, bold, stylized face—a face of
constancy that represents the spiritual base of
society. This head with two faces looking in
opposite directions represents the "inner face"
(*oju inu*), the ancestral bedrock upon which all
of life's temporal transformations take place.

Epa masquerades are staged to remember the
achievements of long-deceased members of the
community. The sculptures depict idealized
individuals who embodied culturally significant
values during their lifetimes. The female figure
emerges last because all society depends upon
woman's power: "It is she who holds within her
womb 'powers concealed' (*egungun*) and the
future promise of community."[8]

Twins are highly symbolic to Yoruba people,
who have the highest twinning rate in the
world. Twins are thought to have superhuman
attributes that can bring both goodness and
evil. Twins are referred to as "two gods, who
entered the world with many followers" and as
"dual spirits ... who open doors on earth and in
heaven."[10] Here, two male twins on their
mother's lap are positioned above two female
figures, also perhaps twins. Just as the female
twins symbolically uphold the male twins, the
males shelter the females by holding either
offering trays or cooling fans above their heads.

Every detail of this sculpture holds meaning.
The mother wears a large brass collar of a
devotee of the goddess, Osun, "owner of all
waters/bestower of children."[11] The hairstyle

worn by the mother and her male twins is a
priestly style called *agogo*. The marks called *pele*
on the cheeks are cosmetic markings that
indicate a high aesthetic consciousness. The
central female is flanked around the base by
another female figure called Olumeye, meaning
"one who knows honor" and referring to a
devotee and messenger of the gods, and by a
male drummer who intones celebratory praises
invoked by this extraordinary work of art.

The sculpture celebrates both the *ase* (life-force)
and *ewa* (beauty) that the gods have bestowed
upon this woman. Yoruba aesthetic concepts
are rich and poetic, with allusion to the inner
and outer aspects of beauty, goodness, and
character (*iwa*), and to the wonder, innovation,
invention, genius, and creativity (*ara*) of the
artist. All of these aspects together make a
masquerade, with its visual and multisensory
elements, a transformative aesthetic experience.

> What do we call food for the eyes?

> What pleases the eyes as prepared yam
> flour satisfies the stomach?

> The eyes have no other food than the
> spectacle. (Adeboye Babalola)[12]

Chapter 1

Faces of Birth and Generation

Female Figure: *Akua ba*

Asante Group, Akan Peoples, Ghana
Late 19th to early 20th century
Wood, beads, glass, string and metal wire; H. 11 1/2 in. (29.2 cm); W. of head 4 1/8 in. (10.5 cm)
Purchased with funds from the Libbey Endowment, Gift of Edward Drummond Libbey, 1989.110

Wednesday's Child

A child is like a rare bird.
A child is precious like coral.
A child is precious like brass.
You cannot buy a child in the market.
Not for all the money in the world.
Only a child brings us joy.
A child is the beginning and
end of happiness.[13]

The importance of children as a source of richness and prosperity in Africa has given rise to art forms for coping with problems of sterility and infant mortality. One of the most poetic of forms is the *akua ba* female figure. The akua ba is a sign of hope, aspiration, wishes, and prayers. It is obtained from a sculptor either by a woman who hopes to conceive, or by one who needs or wants added protection during her pregnancy.

The form of the akua ba is one of utmost simplicity and elegant minimalism. A large flat round head surmounts what is usually a simple stick-like form with arms, but no legs. The figures generally have stylized facial features and adornments of beads around the neck, waist, and sometimes the wrists and ears. Here, the figure is more elaborate, possessing an entire body. Such complete forms arc rare, and this one bears a striking resemblance to one in the Metropolitan Museum of Art (inv. no. 1979.206.75) that was probably made by the same artist. The figure has delicate asymmetrical beautification marks on the cheeks and an unusual geometric design on the back of the head, which may relate to a hairstyle pattern or to a protective symbol. The complete figure may have been a commission from a wealthy patron, for example, a diviner or a chief.[14]

Once the figure was sculpted, a woman was to treat the figure as if it were alive. She was to carry it as all young children are carried, on her back, tucked into her wrapper with just the head appearing above the cloth. She was told to feed the figure, bathe it, sleep with it, and give it gifts — such as waist beads and beaded earrings and necklaces. In addition to its instrumentality, the figure also upholds Asante ideals of beauty, health, and goodness in the high round forehead and the finely detailed coiffure.

Akua ba is such a popular image that it has become an iconic signifier both of Ghanaian nationalism and of Africa itself. Akua bas have been placed on Ghanaian stamps, Smithsonian parade floats, American greeting cards, and in many contemporary art forms. There is some speculation as to the formal resemblance that akua ba have to the ancient Egyptian hieroglyph for the key of life.[15]

Akua ba figures and other offerings in a public shrine to Tano, a river or water deity. Photo: Herbert M. Cole, 1976.

Gèlèdé Society Helmet Mask
Yoruba Peoples, Ketu Region,
Republic of Benin
Early to mid 20th century
Wood, paint; H. 20 in. (50.8 cm)
Purchased with funds from the
Libbey Endowment, Gift of
Edward Drummond Libbey,
1970.52

Our Mothers

Those who have children, may their children live to old age.
May the pregnant ones deliver safely. May our elders live long.
The one with the beautiful eyes. "My Mother" of mothers
Who kills stealthily, and walks surreptitiously.
"My Mother" of mothers,
The entire community is in your hands.
(Fayomi, 1982)[17]

M
nurt
warl
cent
king
his r
the t
king
reign
speci
gave
indep
This
Obas
woma
embo
Quee

Upon
establi
withir
head c
wearir
coral c
to the
thus re
semici
behind

Yoruba peoples apply human characteristics to all aspects of existence through metaphors of the face, for the face has the power to embody mysteries. A finely delineated female head surmounted by the scene of a blacksmith's workshop is the subject of this powerful mask, once used in performances by members of the Yoruba Gèlèdé Society. The Gèlèdé spectacle is a public display of colorful masks danced by men to propitiate elderly, ancestral, or deified women thought to possess heightened spiritual knowledge who are called "our mothers." Their transcendent power and supreme life force (*ase*) can unfold both positively in the mystical creation and nurturing of life and negatively in destructive and nefarious witchcraft. Yoruba men stage these masquerades both to celebrate and to placate "our mothers."

All Gèlèdé masks consist of a regal human face, "the face of equanimity,"[18] surmounted by a tray that serves as a stage for projecting the ideals of the Gèlèdé society. The variety of Gèlèdé imagery is dazzling, and often serves as social commentary. Different Gèlèdé societies compete to invent the most innovative and relevant mask forms. In this case, the scene within the house depicts a blacksmith at work

with his assistants. While Gèlèdé masks honor all the professions, metalworking is a highly charged metaphor for concepts of birth and generation, for blacksmiths are considered to be masters of transformation and metamorphosis. Their ability to change raw metal into useful weapons and tools is often compared with the act of creation itself, a process almost as magical and mystical as birth itself, the secret of which belongs to women alone.

The contribution of iron to human civilization is evident in one Yoruba narrative which recounts that when the gods first arrived on earth, the primeval forest was so dense as to be impenetrable, but Ogun (Lord of Iron) used his iron cutlass to cut a path through it.[19] As such, Ogun's iron has enabled humanity to "transform the face of the earth" and "to give the earth a cultured face."[20] Interestingly, Ogun is also responsible for the cosmetic markings that identify cultivated Yoruba people: "Ogun makes the *pele* marks on my face. Ogun makes the *abaja* marks on my cheeks."[21] Due to their wondrous powers, blacksmiths are "the 'children' of the mothers [who] are believed to possess a spiritual life force (ase) equal or superior to that of the deities."[22]

Colorful Gèlèdé masks from Ibòòrò with superstructures in the form of elephants, a lion, and an airplane to signify political might, royal power, and modern technology, respectively, in honor of "our mothers." Photo: Courtesy of Babatunde Lawal, 1982.

Chapter 2

Faces of Community and Cosmos

Initiation Mask: Kabemba
Temne Peoples, Sierra Leone
19th to early 20th century
Wood with applied and incised
sheet copper; H. 20 in. (50.8 cm)
Purchased with funds from the
Libbey Endowment, Gift of
Edward Drummond Libbey,
1964.55

Boys to Men

It is the East that has power. We get sun
from the East, and all other good things.
It is from the East that the
ancestors came.
(Temne saying)[33]

Many faces in the Toledo Museum's African collection are masks associated with preparing youth for adulthood and reinforcing societal values through education, entertainment, historical commentary, social control, litigation, and commemoration of ancestral and larger spiritual forces. Traditional education in rural Africa often involved a series of rites that transformed young girls and boys into women and men, respectively, while also teaching a sense of moral strength and values as well as an appreciation and respect for the generations of ancestors who preceded the living on earth.

Temne Kabemba masks served to reinforce links between initiation and chieftaincy, and between the living and the dead during male initiation rites that included circumcision and the acquisition of secret, esoteric knowledge. Among Temne peoples, initiation is referred to as "the kingdom (Räbai) of Temne, in which young males (*ambai*) are 'crowned' into manhood in a metaphoric parallel to royal coronation."[34] The central spirit figure during the rites is a mask called Kabemba, meaning "ancestor," that is owned by the circumciser but is danced by another official. Kabemba is a benevolent spirit, who acts as a spiritual midwife, leading the boys on the seventh day to the riverside for their ritual washing and the application of protective substances to their

bodies. Water is a symbol of birth from which the neophytes struggle to free themselves and appears in songs throughout the initiation:

When I shall see water
My mind will hang like a life-buoy,
Let them go tell my mother;
Tomorrow we must go to the river.
(Temne song)[35]

The copper and/or brass strip decoration is the distinguishing feature of Kabemba masks. The strips, cut with triangular motifs, are incised and stamped with circle and wave patterns said to be purely decorative, although deeper layers of meaning must not be excluded. In this area indigenous writing systems existed prior to colonialism and were used by the Poro secret association as a means of transmitting arcane knowledge.

The copious use of metal may relate to the metaphor of chieftaincy, for those who have successfully passed into manhood are referred to as "chiefs" and carry staffs that mimic the form of the paramount chief's staff. The gleaming, radiant face of Kabemba, the ancestral spirit presiding over the initiation, reminds the young novices of the larger visage of society and spirituality in which they view their own reflections.[36]

Initiates rehearsing songs and dances during a Räbai initiation among the Temne of Sierra Leone. An unfinished Kabemba mask is held up before an initiate's face, while a dramatic Katomla fiber mask stands behind. Seven initiates stand before the initiation residence in the sacred grove. In the foreground, the master of initiation (Semamasa) leads the singing while an initiate (Sema) beats on his bamboo gong. Photo: Frederick Lamp, 1976.

Helmet Mask: Bwoom

Kuba Peoples, Democratic
Republic of Congo

Late 19th century

Wood, leather, brass, fabric,
cowrie shells, and beads; H. 25 in.
(63.5 cm)

Purchased with funds from the
Libbey Endowment, Gift of
Edward Drummond Libbey,
1970.18

King and Commoner

It is not I who created your title. It is
your God who arranged it from before
your birth, that you would hold this title.
I am like the messenger of God [...].
Kingship is not a thing of the Crown
Council. Kingship. God created it.
(Kuba King talking to his
titleholder in 1953)[37]

This mask, with its massive proportions and powerful features, is a historical archive. For Kuba peoples, history is an important intellectual activity and the most ancient histories are considered to be the most prestigious. History is not only preserved and transmitted through oral traditions, but also through masquerade performances during which significant historical episodes are reenacted. In this sense, masks are memory devices to stimulate remembrance of the past in ways that are relevant to the present. From the seventeenth to nineteenth centuries, the Kuba were organized as a confederation of more than seventeen ethnic groups united under the aegis of a lineage of kings from the Bushoong dynasty.

This mask once formed part of a triad of masks that was danced at initiations, funerals, and other public ceremonies to dramatize the origins of Kuba kingship and to celebrate the culture heroes of Kuba society. Called Bwoom, this large helmet mask was second in the hierarchy after the king's mask, Mwash aMbooy (see p. 57), which symbolizes both the creator ancestor, Woot, and an elder of great wisdom and experience. The third mask in the trilogy is a female mask, Ngady mwaash, which may depict the king's sister-consort with whom the king is said to have had incestuous relations that gave birth to humanity. Bwoom is variously described as a commoner, a

prince, or a subversive element at court who competes with Mwash aMbooy for the love of Ngady mwaash. Whereas the mask to represent Woot is worn by the king and buried with him at death, the Bwoom mask is kept by royal lineages as a permanent symbol of family continuity.[38]

Explanations for Bwoom's pronounced forehead state that it depicts a prince with a genetic trait called steeple skull, or the head of a Tshwa Pygmy. Tshwa were the first inhabitants of the area and still continue to recognize their rights. It is possible that the mask represented conflicts between ruling elites and native peoples who preceded Kuba kingship.

The mask's forehead and mouth are covered with leaves of metal, and metal strips delineate the cheekbones. Cowries and beads accentuate the bold volumes of the mask, which would have been worn with a dramatic costume of a painted raffia tunic with fresh cut leaves around the hips. Feathers were probably attached to the top of the head, and parrot feathers were affixed under the chin, while the entire outfit was adorned with fluttering yellow palm fronds.

Bwoom masks generally perform exuberantly, but with carefully executed dance steps that tell stories and recall past events for audience members who recognize the historical allusions with communal pride and satisfaction.[39]

Bwoom dances with Mwash aMbooy, the king's mask, in a historical dramatization of power relationships that helps spectators to recall significant events of the Kuba past. Photo: A. Turconi, 1974, courtesy of Joseph Cornet and Monni Adams.

Rainbow Mask
Baule or Yaure Peoples, Ivory Coast
Early to mid 20th century
Wood, metal plates, metal tacks;
H. 17 3/4 in. (45.1 cm)
Purchased with funds from the
Libbey Endowment, Gift of
Edward Drummond Libbey,
1973.12

Warming the Dance Space

A common nickname for the most beloved masks is *alie kora*, meaning "dinner is burning," because these masks almost always appear late in the day, and women who rush to watch them often abandon their cooking.[55]

This humorous anecdote provides a glimpse into the popularity of mask performances among Baule peoples, some of which are designed for the pure pleasure ("sweetness") and joy of entertainment. Yet, entertainment has a deeper meaning than pure distraction. Baule peoples derive an indescribable sense of satisfaction and pride from the collective endeavors that masquerades represent. Entertainment-mask performances provide psychological relief in times of social stress and impart a sense of security and well-being to all members of the community.[56]

Masquerades are not a static medium. Rather, they are genres like opera and film noir, whose contents, scripts, and actors change over time and are continually reinvented to meet changing social circumstances. One masquerade called Gbagba, which has undergone considerable modification since the early twentieth century, can be described as a microcosm of the human world, with a meaningful hierarchical system that alludes to the great dichotomies of Baule life: village and wilderness, women and men. The masks appear in a sequence that begins with human types, such as the foreign Fulani woman or the prostitute; animals, such as the baboon, antelope, and buffalo; and natural phenomena

such as the moon or the rainbow, as is probably depicted by this mask. The role of these first masks is to "warm the dance space" and to prepare the arena for the next and more prestigious portrait masks.

The form and the style of this mask suggest that it may be the work of an artist who sculpted masks in the courtyard of the National Museum of Ivory Coast in the 1940s and 1950s.[57] It is not clear whether he was of Yaure or Baule origin, and his name is unknown. This artist produced a vast corpus of masks both for local and foreign consumption, and he also had followers who copied his style. The artist's hand is especially recognizable in the rendering of the eyebrows and the nose. The mask reflects an overall attempt to achieve beauty and skillfulness of form—the ultimate goals of Baule aesthetic philosophy.

Between dances, masks are kept out of sight, not only to protect them from public view and insect damage but also to increase the aesthetic impact of the mask when it does appear. As one Baule person said, "You have to keep it hidden someplace a long time so that the day you take it out, people think it is beautiful. The less you dance it, the more people appreciate it. If you see it every day, you will not think it is beautiful any more" (Kami, 1996).[58]

A horned mask performing for a Gbagba-type dance in Kongonou village, Aitu area, Ivory Coast. Photo: Susan M. Vogel, 1978.

Chapter 3

Faces of Honor and Prestige

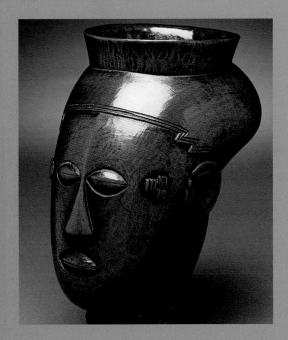

Pendant
Baule Peoples, Ivory Coast
Early 20th century
Cast and tooled gold; H. 1 15/16 in.
(5 cm), W. 1 3/4 in. (4.5 cm)
Purchased with funds from the
Libbey Endowment, Gift of
Edward Drummond Libbey,
1977.72

Like a God

Gold gives force. If it has no power, it is not real gold. That is why all important things include gold....When an important person dies, gold honors the deceased; these honors are only for important people…. Gold brings strength, but it is also given to [produce] calm…. Gold calms evil spirits.

(Kami, 1993)[59]

While one might think of gold ornaments as a symbol of wealth in the material sense, Baule people ascribe a far more sacred value to this precious metal. For them, gold is "like a god" and is treated as an heirloom that evokes the presence of the ancestors. Baule families keep gold in ancestral treasuries called *aja*, which contain assorted prestige articles, including solid cast gold ornaments; carved wooden objects with gold foil, such as fly whisks and swords; as well as gold nuggets and gold dust wrapped in textiles or guarded in packets, bundles, and suitcases. As a unit, the aja represents the "force of the ancestors" and serves as the "soul" of the family.[60]

A finely cast gold pendant in the form of a man's face would once have belonged to such a treasury. It is a work of remarkable precision and delicacy, with a finely delineated beard and exquisitely rendered hair and eyebrows. The raised designs between the eyes and in front of the ears are cosmetic marks of Baule identity, and the entire piece conveys a love for gold that transcends its materiality. Here, affection for the medium is manifest in the intricate detailing of form and the graceful simplification of facial features. The intimate size and dimensions of the pendant gives it the personal aura of a locket or an antique pocket watch.

The contents of an aja treasury are treated with extraordinary reverence, for they are considered to be protected by supernatural sanctions. They must never be altered or reconstituted by succeeding generations. Anyone who steals, removes, trades, or recombines objects in the treasury is subject to the ancestors' wrath. It is conceivable that the casting flaw under this man's nose might be the reason why the pendant's owner or artist was willing to relinquish it.

Only a few occasions sanction the public display of gold. Important funerals call for a show of the wealth from different related families. Worked gold ornaments are laid out around the body of the deceased in order to "give honor to your family, and to express condolences." After the funeral, the objects are returned to their owners. A second context for the display of gold is a ceremony to mark the end of mourning, when a widow is elegantly bedecked in fine cloth and gold ornaments before returning them to their sacred treasury.[61]

A Baule chief and his retinue in full regalia, including gold-covered fly whisks, lanterns, knives, swords, and pendants, in Golikro village, Aitu area, Ivory Coast. Photo: Susan M. Vogel, 1982.

Vessel: *Kuduo*

Asante Group, Akan Peoples, Ghana

18ᵗʰ to 19ᵗʰ century

Cast and raised copper alloy;
H. 8 ⁵/₈ in. (21.9 cm), W. 6 ⁵/₈ in.
(16.8 cm)

Purchased with funds from the
Libbey Endowment, Gift of
Edward Drummond Libbey,
1994.23

Soul's Basin

A hungry leopard tries to eat any animal.
The rain wets the spots on the leopard's
skin but does not wash them off.
(Akan proverbs)[62]

Cast by the lost-wax method, this *kuduo* represents centuries of cultural and religious interaction and synthesis in the region that is now Ghana. Kuduo vessels, which were used in a wide variety of ritual contexts by Akan peoples until the early twentieth century, have antecedents in Islamic basins that were imported into the region in the fourteenth and fifteenth centuries from Egypt and the Near East. It is likely that Dyula (Islamized Mande peoples) traders purchased or traded such vessels at trade cities in the western Sudan, such as Djenne and Timbuktu, and brought them back to Ghana where they were assimilated and reproduced over the centuries.[63] Kuduo were made until the late nineteenth century, when the changes associated with colonialism proved so overwhelming that many older traditions were abandoned. Production of kuduo recommenced in the 1920s and 1930s when artists began to cast them for Europeans.

This excellent precolonial example is a "casket kuduo" that could be locked and was made for storing precious items, such as gold dust, gold weights, beads, and pendants. Since both gold weights and kuduo are associated with a person's soul, they were buried together with the deceased. Kuduo served many other functions, such as the presentation of offerings to the spirits of deceased ancestors and deities, in the rites to ensure a newborn's good health, for girls' puberty rites, and during royal purification rites, in which the king and his sub-chiefs used the receptacle for sacred water.[64]

Two salient features of this kuduo are its beautifully inscribed surface and the animal imagery on its lid. The geometric, seemingly decorative motifs arranged in horizontal bands around the surface of the vessel derive from the earliest documented Islamic basins, which were covered with Arabic script or in some cases with arabesque. In this case, the artist may have been unfamiliar with Arabic language, but he faithfully imitated the pervasive inscriptions through intricate designs and patterns, such as scallops, lotus forms, and waving lines that give the effect of writing.

Complementing these Islamic influences, a characteristically Akan motif surmounts the kuduo's lid—the image of two animals in mortal combat. A leopard attacks a horned quadruped that is probably an antelope. Such scenes in Akan visual arts almost always refer to verbal proverbs that Akan peoples value highly and which usually have a moral message. Here, it is probable that the rapaciousness of the leopard, which kills for pure pleasure, is a positive political statement about ruthless power and may be a metaphor for Akan incursions into the Ghanaian north.[65]

Palm Wine Cup
Kuba Peoples, Democratic
Republic of Congo
Early 20th century
Wood; H. 6 15/32 in. (16.4 cm)
Purchased with funds from the
Florence Scott Libbey Bequest in
Memory of her Father, Maurice
A. Scott, 1991.55

Vessel of Wisdom

Sweet youth lacks wisdom, wise old age
lacks sweetness of character.
(Kuba proverb)[66]

Palm wine is so central to Kuba life as a social, ritual, and ceremonial beverage that it provides apt metaphors for human behavior and development. Palm wine is collected early in the day, at which time it has a sweet and mild flavor. Over the course of the day it ferments, becoming stronger and more pungent, as well as more intoxicating. In this and other regions of central Africa, palm wine plays an important role in social life, as a focal point around which discussions, conversations, and palavers take place.

In the precolonial period, Kuba titleholders and other high-ranking officials drank palm wine from sculpted wooden cups in the form of human heads or full human bodies. The cups also served as display pieces. The faces are not intended as portraits of specific individuals, although they convey important information about identity. The hairline shown on this head is quintessentially Kuba. It is a style that was worn by men and women in the nineteenth and early twentieth centuries by shaving a straight hairline with a curved or chiseled angle at the temples. The marks in front of each ear are scarification patterns, serving both as protective devices and as marks of Kuba social identity.[67]

Kuba peoples are known for their elaborate and sometimes sumptuous manufacture of even mundane articles, such as cosmetic boxes and trumpets, pipes and drums. The idea of sculpting a drinking vessel as a human head is not only a reflection of the wealth and status of the owner but also had ritual overtones. Among neighboring Luba peoples to the east, the transmission of power to a new king required consumption of human blood mixed with palm wine from the dried cranium of his predecessor. The head was considered to be the locus of power and wisdom, and blood was the sacrificial agent that rendered a king semi-divine. Eventually, Luba sculpted heads replaced actual crania, which leads one to wonder if Kuba cups might have had a parallel development. In any event, such cups would never have been used in public by the highest ranking members in the Kuba hierarchy, who were required to drink and eat in total privacy, away from public view.[68]

The simplicity of the cup's lines and the elegance of its form are accentuated by the richness of its deep red tone—the result of applications of *tool*, a red powder made from ground camwood and palm oil that Kuba people also apply to their own skin. Certain elements make this cup distinctive, such as the way the neckband becomes the handle as one turns the cup around and the rendering of ears as simple concentric circles, a symbol that may relate to genealogy and ancestry.

*A titled Kuba official drinking from a carved wooden cup.
Photo: Joseph Cornet, 1974, courtesy of Monni Adams.*

Horse and Rider
Yoruba Peoples, Republic of Benin
Early 20th century
Wood; H. 17 ³/₄ in. (45.1 cm),
L. 15 ¹/₈ in. (38.4 cm)
Purchased with funds from the
Libbey Endowment, Gift of
Edward Drummond Libbey,
1973.11

One Who Rides Fire

They say that fire kills water.
He rides fire like a horse.
Lightning—with what kind of cloth
do you cover your body?
With the cloth of death.
(Yoruba poem)[69]

The mounted leader is one of the most prevalent themes in African art, both for historical and symbolic reasons.[70] In Yoruba sculpture, images of riders support Ifa divination bowls, appear among the hierarchical compositions of house posts, surmount Epa helmet masks, and adorn shrines. In a general sense, the equestrian is a symbol of power, for to ride a horse implies both wealth and elevated status. In a more specifically historical sense, the equestrian refers to the important roles of cavalries in Oyo kings' campaigns from the sixteenth to eighteenth centuries. In the late eighteenth and nineteenth centuries, only Yoruba chiefs and their retainers were privileged to own and ride horses, but the theme has remained in Yoruba art as a rich metaphor for ideas about status, control, and access to supernatural powers.

Some Yoruba gods are represented through riding metaphors, such as Shango, the God of Thunder and Lightning, who is called "he who rides fire like a horse." A Yoruba myth features the horse as a source of competition and conflict. It recounts that Obatala, the god who creates all human bodies, was returning from a long journey and saw a great white stallion, which he decided to ride the remaining distance to the capital. The horse belonged to Shango, who, when he heard that someone had ridden it, ordered Obatala to be imprisoned, even though the elderly gods had sent

their apologies to the king. As the days and months passed, the rains failed and drought spread through the land. The earth became parched and women ceased to give birth. Only when pleas from his chiefs convinced Shango to release the creator God, did the rains return so life could be resuscitated. Such stories articulate a deeply felt ambivalence about power, both political and psychological.[71]

The God Ogun, God of Iron and Warfare, is also implicit to equestrian images associated with warfare. Ogun as a symbol of political and social mobility, represents both the change and transformation effected by conquest and battle, as well as the mobility of the gods. When a god comes to mount the head of an adept through spirit possession (*gun*), the adept is literally and figuratively said "to be ridden" (*ele gun*).[72] Worshippers are known as "gods' mounts" or "horses of the gods."[73]

This horse and rider is unusual for its active composition. Most *ele sin* equestrians are shown in a stationary or supportive mode. The animation of this sculpture may reflect Fon influence, a group that blends with Yoruba culture in the Republic of Benin.[74] It is likely that this figure was once used to enrich a shrine dedicated to the protection of warriors. The top of the rider's head looks as though it may have supported a bowl for offerings to the gods.

The Yoruba say that "proverbs are the horses of speech" (*owe, l'esin oro*). In other words, proverbs are succinct verbal evocations and embellishments of conversation that support, carry, and elevate speech and intensify the expressiveness of ideas. Proverbs are verbal art, not simply verbal communication. Thus we may understand Yoruba arts as embellishments that uplift and move their viewers by the beauty and power of their expressiveness.[75]

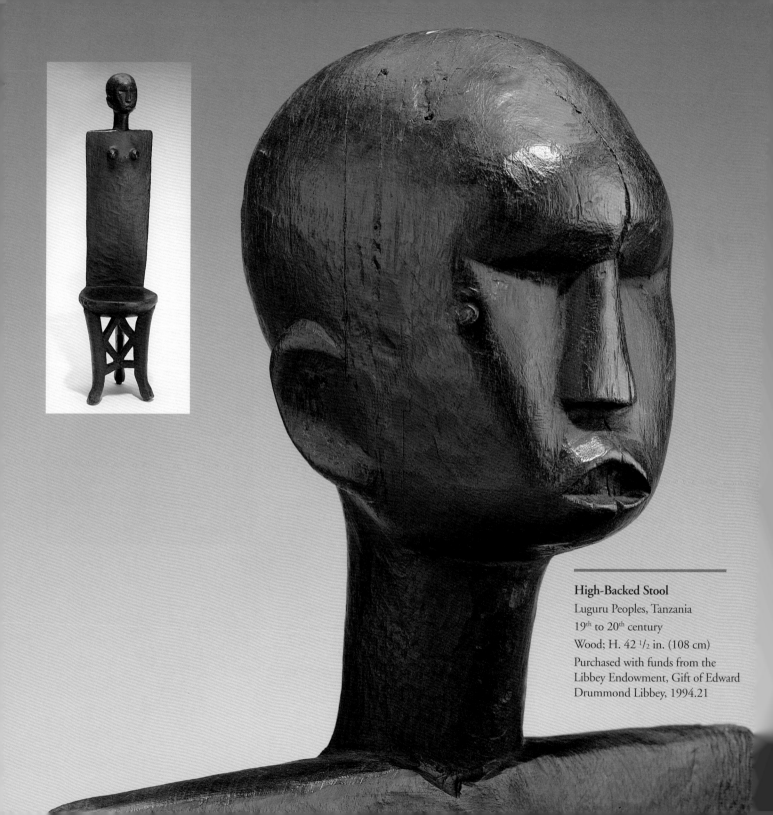

High-Backed Stool
Luguru Peoples, Tanzania
19th to 20th century
Wood; H. 42 1/2 in. (108 cm)
Purchased with funds from the
Libbey Endowment, Gift of Edward
Drummond Libbey, 1994.21

Seat of Embrace

Interacting, man and symbol achieve a higher existence than either could reach alone. Together they can transform ordinary time and ordinary space into an extraordinary event.[76]

T hroughout Africa, sculpted stools are not only thrones for sitting but also metaphorical seats of sacred authority and royal power. In Tanzania and eastern Congo, a "high-backed stool" was the emblem of choice for a number of chieftaincies, including Tabwa, Nyamwezi, Luguru, and Hehe peoples, in the late nineteenth and early twentieth centuries. Stools in this particular cross-cultural tradition differ from those of other parts of Africa in that they have a high back, similar to a chair with no arms.[77]

Even more striking, however, is that the back is often carved with the characteristics of a woman, with breasts protruding from the plank against which one would have leaned one's back. The implication of the design is that the chair is a seat of "embrace," in which a chief becomes fused with a symbol of his maternal line of descent. In fact, Nyamwezi peoples refer to their mothers' male kin as "the back," in reference to the way that small children are carried on their mothers' backs.[78]

There is some speculation as to whether people ever sat on such stools. A hole in the center of the seat of many related examples, and a hollow cylindrical tube below that hole under the seat, leads one to suspect that a pole or some other implement was used to raise the seat for carrying in processions.[79]

The Toledo stool reflects a blending of peoples in this region, for while the head and the base of the stool both appear to be Luguru in style, its facial features share similarities with Nyamwesi peoples. The elegant designs on the back are similar to coastal Swahili artists' use of chip-carved design motifs on commemorative posts and doors.[80]

Yet the actual design produced by the chip-carving technique on this stool is identical to a highly symbolic motif of isosceles triangles found on Tabwa high-backed stools and other chieftainly emblems and is called *balamwezi*, "the rising of a new moon." For Tabwa peoples, who reside in eastern Congo along the shores of Lake Tanganyika, the moon is a symbol of hope, rejuvenation, and rebirth, and such stools are made to reinforce and consolidate power and to symbolize the chief's elevated status.[81] But the high-backed stool also serves to give concrete form to the notion of ancestral support, for by sitting upon one's ancestor, one is literally upheld by the deeds of one's forebears and reminded of one's responsibility to maintain social health and prosperity.[82]

45

Chapter 4

Faces of
Spirit and Soul

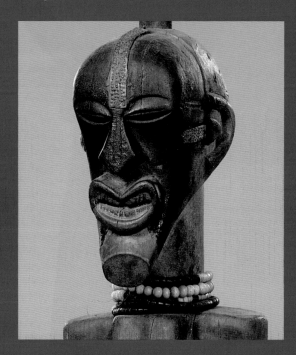

Power Figure: *Nkishi*

Songye Peoples, Democratic
Republic of Congo

Mid 19th to early 20th century

Wood, metal, beads, woven grass,
antelope horn; H. 41 in. (104.2 cm)

Purchased with funds from the
Libbey Endowment, Gift of
Edward Drummond Libbey,
1970.51

A Hiding Place for the Soul

Nkishi is the name of things we use to help a man when he is sick and from which we obtain health. Nkishi protects people's souls and guards against illness. Thus nkishi is something that hunts down illness and chases it away from the body. In nkishi also is the safe upbringing of children. It is a hiding place for people's souls, to keep and compose in order to preserve life. Everybody is very grateful to *minkishi* [plural] for helping them. (Nsemi)[98]

A looming presence, this robust figure once served an entire community in times of need for protection, healing, and therapy. Although sculpted by a wood carver, the actual "artist" of the work was an *nganga*, or ritual specialist, who empowered the object through the addition of magical substances (*bishimba*) inside cavities in the head and abdomen. Nkishi figures were of essentially two types, those intended to counteract malevolent forces and those destined to attract positive effects;[99] it is no longer possible to say which purpose was served by this figure. Such figures were valued by Songye peoples not primarily on the basis of outward form and sculptural quality but rather on the effectiveness of their aid. In other words, Songye aesthetic judgments rest not only on how an object looks but on its capacity to "work."[100]

The bishimba cannot be seen, for they are inside the horn surmounting the head and, probably, in the abdomen behind the metal stud that seals the passageway of the navel. This stud serves to seal in powers that are ultimately to be released for mystical purposes. Other elements are added to augment the visual impact of the nkishi, such as beads and a raffia skirt that would have been the apparel of a chief. The copper strips on the forehead and at the temples are references to lightning,[101] while the bushbuck antelope horn is a common receptacle in central Africa for holding medicines, and also signals the aggression encompassed by this highly charged figure.[102] Such figures were considered to be so powerful that they were handled by long sticks and never with the bare hands.

The figure is a monument to geometric thrust. It speaks to its viewer as if to menace, threaten, or intimidate. And yet, it also demands to be looked at; it has an exacting presence through the power of its volumetric form. The figure leans forward at an angle as if to approach its beholder, and with bared teeth and hands akimbo, almost seems to be in motion. Indeed, among neighboring Luba peoples, a horn in the top of such a figure gives the object the power of locomotion.[103]

Nkishi figures and related power objects are used throughout the Bantu-speaking region, among Kongo, Kuba, and Luba, as well as by peoples of African descent in the Americas. The concept of nkishi also inspires the art of contemporary artists such as Renée Stout, who makes nkishis as a form of healing and personal transformation.[104]

Headdress: Mukenga

Kuba Peoples, Democratic
Republic of Congo

Early 20th century

Raffia, wood, beads, shells, leopard
skin, palm fibers; H. 21 3/4 in
(55.3 cm), W 13 1/8 in. (33.3 cm)

Purchased with funds from the
Libbey Endowment, Gift of
Edward Drummond Libbey,
1973.13

King of the Elephants

An animal, even if it is large, does not
surpass the elephant.
A man, even if he has authority, does not
surpass the king.
(Kuba proverb)[105]

Facing death is the theme of Kuba masquerades staged for deceased members of the men's initiation society among the Bushoong, Shoowa, and many other groups in the northern half of the Kuba kingdom. While all funerals are important, those of chiefs, titleholders, and other members of aristocratic clans are critical events to society as a whole. They are occasions for mourning and celebration, as well as contexts for lavish displays of insignia, dress, and accouterments that reflect histories of trade, economic hegemony, and political domination.

During the nineteenth century, Kuba rulers gained control of elephant herds and traded ivory through long-distance networks. This activity brought great wealth and established the Kuba as a regional power. As a result of the political consolidation and enormous monetary gains of this period, elephants and ivory came to be associated with paramount rulers (*nyim*) and their titleholders. The Mukenga headdress is a remarkable rendering of rulership in the form of an elephant. During the masquerade performance, the dancer wearing the Mukenga mask personifies an important titleholder dancing to honor the deceased.[106]

The high projecting "trunk" of this headdress is the most obvious reference to the mightiest of beasts, and many Mukenga masks also have decorated tusks. But the animal imagery is not restricted to the elephant. The face is covered with the fur of a spotted cat, such as a serval—a symbol of titleholders in the service of the chief—and white cowrie shells. Cowries are among the most visible objects of wealth displayed at funerals. They are placed on the ankles and arms of the deceased and are included in the inventory of burial goods.[107] A spectacular white outfit covered with cowries is the most important garment owned by a king and is worn only on the days of his investiture and his funeral. White cowries indicate that a ruler or other officeholder is descended from Woot, the founding ancestor of Kuba culture who came from the sea.[108]

The Mukenga headdress not only dances at funerals but also forms part of the funerary dress of deceased titleholders. Among neighboring Ndengese peoples, following the death of a senior titleholder, an effigy of the deceased is crowned with the Mukenga mask. His successor is made to spend a period of time facing the effigy to transfer power from the dead to the living.[109] Death is never an end in itself in Africa. It signals new beginnings, continuities, and strong and resilient responses on the part of communities that consolidate in times of stress to bring change and transformation of the most positive sort.

Like Mukenga, this Mwash aMbooy masquerade represents elite leadership. Whereas Mukenga has an elephant trunk projecting from the head to signify paramount rulership, Mwash aMbooy has a shock of eagle feathers on his head as a symbol of power and connection to the founding ancestor of the Kuba kingdom. Photo: A. Turconi, 1974, courtesy of Joseph Cornet and Monni Adams.

Mask: *Ngontang*
Fang Peoples, Gabon
Late 19th century
Wood, pigment; H. 17 in. (43.2 cm),
W. 11 ¹/₂ in. (29.2 cm)
Purchased with funds from the
Libbey Endowment, Gift of
Edward Drummond Libbey,
1958.16

Another Other World

Ngontang is the mask of the "young white woman," a spirit who has returned from the land of the dead, the other world across the seas—in the country of the Europeans.[110]

This mask is derived from a type called *ngontang*, formerly used by Fang peoples to celebrate the visitation of spirits upon the living.[111] This particular example, however, was probably never used by Fang peoples themselves. In a somewhat ironic twist of fate, this mask—which was probably made before 1900 as part of a group for sale to foreigners—came into the possession of two early Modernist European artists, Maurice Vlaminck and André Derain, whose work was influenced by African sculpture in transforming and enduring ways.

Derain's diary describes how he and Vlaminck were sitting in a bar outside Paris in 1905 when a trader came in with two almost identical wood masks from what was then French Equatorial Africa. The two men were so impressed with the works of art that they purchased them. It is not clear whether Derain bought one and Vlaminck the other, or whether Vlaminck bought both and later sold one to Derain. But it is certain that Vlaminck owned this mask before 1937, when it was sold at an auction of Vlaminck's collection at the Hôtel Drouot. The other mask is now in the Musée National d'Art Moderne, Paris, and Derain is known to have made a bronze casting of it, which is in the Musée des Arts Africains et Océaniens, Paris.[112]

Throughout Bantu-speaking regions of central Africa, whiteness is associated with death and otherworldiness and, more generally, with states of transition and transformation. The whiteness of this mask type represented the otherness of the spirit world for Fang peoples even before it came to be associated with Europeans. African masks, in turn, became a symbol of African otherness for European artists of the early twentieth century who found in African art a new sensibility and an inspirational approach to perception and representation.

While the influence of African art on early Modern art cannot be underestimated, it must be remembered that African art was appreciated and borrowed by early Modernists only for its formal attributes, with little understanding of the principles underlying its outward appearance. In the decades since Vlaminck, Derain, and Picasso, African art has come to hold a place of its own in the history of art, without ignoring the interconnectedness of different cultural aesthetics.

This portrait of Paul Guillaume, a Parisian art dealer who sold African objects as well as the work of Max Jacob, Constantin Brancusi, and Amedeo Modigliani, is an example of African influence on early twentieth century European painting. Guillaume's face is shown as if it were a Fang mask, with sharply defined flat surfaces and eyes that resemble cut-out openings. Amedeo Modigliani (Italian, 1884–1920), Portrait of Paul Guillaume, *1915. Oil on board, 29 1/2 x 20 1/2 in. (74.9 x 52.1 cm). Gift of Mrs. C. Lockhart McKelvy, 1951.382.*

Reliquary Figure

Kota Peoples, Gabon

Late 19th to early 20th century

Wood covered with brass, copper, and iron sheeting; H. 20 in. (50.8 cm), W. 11 3/4 in. (29.8 cm)

Purchased with funds from the Libbey Endowment, Gift of Edward Drummond Libbey, 1973.10

Face of the *Bwiti*

To be and become, to live and die are
but two faces of the same reality.[113]

The faces of Janus figures and masks
look backward and forward, from
defective past to perfected future—just as
Janus was the ancient Roman god of
thresholds and passages.[114]

I t is fitting that an object intended to
memorialize the dead should be janiform,
or double, with faces looking in both
directions, to the past and the future, to the
world of the living and that of the dead.
Although no longer used today, the purpose
of such reliquary figures was to protect a basket
or bark box containing the skulls, bones, and
other relics of important deceased ancestors,
such as former chiefs, lineage heads, artists,
judges, and especially fecund women. The
figure was lashed to the container through the
lozenge base that doubled as an abbreviated
body. The copper, while brilliant and valuable,
also imparted an aura that may have been
repellent to trespassers who might dare enter
the sanctuary without authorization.[115]

Kota figures have many different appearances.
They are usually singled-faced, with a smaller
number of Janus sculptures.[116] The two faces
on this reliquary guardian differ considerably.
One side has a large protruding forehead,
round eyes, and a linear design of horizontal
metal strips on the cheeks that contrasts with
the smoothly curving surface of the forehead.
The other has a slightly concave surface with
diagonal strips radiating in opposite directions
on the cheeks and above the eyes. Perhaps the
two faces were an added protection, to watch

in both directions. More likely, however, the
two faces simply displayed more wealth. The
metal used to cover the wood core of Kota
sculptures was taken from materials coming
into Equatorial Africa through European
colonialism and trade, such as brass ingots,
copper vessels, and wire that were beaten,
flattened and stretched over the surface in an
ostentatious show of wealth. Such figures were
sometimes removed from their places atop the
reliquaries to be used in public performances.
The two faces undoubtedly augmented the
sculpture's theatrical effect.[117]

Kota peoples claim that the sculpture depicted
the actual skulls inside the baskets. Both the
skulls and the reliquary guardian figures were
publicly displayed during funerals, before a
communal hunt, or at the onset of an
epidemic. The figures were offered sacrifices,
and during initiation rites called *bwiti*, the
novices' fathers danced with the "face of the
bwiti," swinging it back and forth in their
hands.[118] The community reaped enormous
stores of power and strength from the sight of
the reliquary guardian. The object was a source
not only of aesthetic delight but also of spiritual
sustenance, for the reliquaries were thought to
retain the powers of the deceased and to bring
their positive influences to surviving kin.

Slit Drum

Mangbetu Peoples, Democratic Republic of Congo

Late 19th to early 20th century

Wood with cast metal rings; H. 11 1/2 in. (29.2 cm), W. 26 1/4 in. (66.7 cm)

Purchased with funds from the Libbey Endowment, Gift of Edward Drummond Libbey, 1983.90

Africa is Calling

When the wind blows into its hollow
body, it lows like a buffalo.[119]

A large bell-shaped object with sleek
contours and minimalist lines, this drum
served as a mouthpiece for an entire community.
The "talking drum" was played to alert the
community to a festival or ceremony, to warn
people away from a sacred precinct, to call men
to war, or to convey news of the king's death.
Made from a dark, hard wood, the drum is
sometimes carved a different thickness on each
side to maximize the number of tonal variations
that can be produced. Through combinations of
high and low tones in long and short sequences,
the slit drum can transmit complex verbal
messages that imitate the sounds of language over
distances of several kilometers.

In addition to their use for communication, such
drums served primarily as a symbol of royal
authority. Kings and paramount chiefs gave them
to lesser chiefs to invest them with power. At the
court, a small drum like this was often paired with
a larger one in the form of a buffalo or a crocodile.
During dances, the drum could be used to
request drinks for musicians, call dancers to the
arena by name, and give instructions to the
performers.

Finally, the drum could announce the arrival of
foreigners. As in many parts of Africa, explorers and
scientific expeditions that came to the area had a
profound influence on Mangbetu culture in the
late nineteenth and early twentieth centuries.

The encounters left a permanent imprint on the
inhabitants, who began to produce works of art
that reflected their interactions with and perceptions of these European and American visitors.

The interface between cultures and continents is
enduring and mutual. As James Clifford has
written, "cultures do not hold still for their
portraits," and as the Mangbetu case demon-
strates, both sides in a face-to-face encounter are
affected and transformed.[120] When we face
another person, we face ourselves, and in that
image we may perceive a familiar reflection. As
Roland Barthes said of Greta Garbo's iconic face,
"the face ... is an idea."[121] And as Susan Stewart
writes, "the face reveals a depth and profundity....
It is a type of 'deep' text, a text whose meaning is
complicated by change and by a constant series of
alternations between a reader and an author who
is strangely disembodied,... but, [who is] in fact
created by this reading."[122]

The slit drum is a reminder that African art is
not silent; it is full of voices waiting to be heard.
African art, culture, and history are an on-going,
living legacy that has a great deal to teach and to
tell. The works in the Toledo Museum collection
summon viewers to share in the brilliance and
poetry of African artistic heritage. To face these
works is to "walk with the elders," for these
are objects that will "open doors on earth and
in heaven."

*Titleholders of the Luba kingdom, another central
African polity, playing a slit drum on the occasion
of a royal celebration. The slit drum summons people
to participation in an uplifting communal endeavor.
Photo: Mary Nooter Roberts, 1989.*

Notes

1 Quoted in Henry John Drewal and John Mason, *Beads, Body, and Soul: Art and Light in the Yoruba Universe,* exhibition catalogue (Los Angeles: UCLA Fowler Museum of Cultural History, 1998) 81.

2 Mary Nooter Roberts and Allen F. Roberts, *Memory: Luba Art and the Making of History,* exhibition catalogue (New York and Munich: The Museum for African Art and Prestel, 1996).

3 Henry John Drewal, John Pemberton III, and Rowland Abiodun, *Yoruba: Nine Centuries of African Art and Thought,* exhibition catalogue (New York: The Center for African Art in association with Harry N. Abrams, Inc., 1989) 26.

4 Ibid., 26, and Robert Farris Thompson, *Face of the Gods: Art and Altars of Africa and the African Americas* (New York and Munich: The Museum for African Art and Prestel, 1993).

5 Babatunde Lawal, "Beyond Physiognomy: The Signifying Face in Yoruba Art and Thought" (forthcoming).

6 John Pemberton III, "The Carvers of the Northeast," in Drewal, Pemberton, and Abiodun 1989 (above n. 3) 202.

7 After Alisa LaGamma, labels for the exhibition "Master Hand: Individuality and Creativity among Yoruba Sculptors," The Metropolitan Museum of Art, New York (September 11, 1997–March 1, 1998).

8 Pemberton 1989 (above n. 6) 197.

9 John Pemberton III and William Fagg, ed. Bryce Holcombe, *Yoruba: Sculpture of West Africa* (New York: Alfred A. Knopf, 1982) 162, 80.

10 Babatunde Lawal, personal communication, 1998.

11 Pemberton 1982 (above n. 9) 198.

12 Quoted in Babatunde Lawal, *The Gèlèdé Spectacle: Art, Gender, and Social Harmony in an African Culture* (Seattle: University of Washington Press, 1996) 98.

13 Yoruba verse, quoted in John Mason, "Old, New World Religion," in *Faces: The Magazine About People* (issue on "The Yoruba People: Nigeria and Beyond") (Peterborough, N.H.: Cobblestone, 1995) 19.

14 Doran H. Ross, personal communication, 1998.

15 Doran H. Ross, "Akua's Child and Other Relatives: New Mythologies for Old Dolls," in *Isn't S/He A Doll: Play and Ritual in African Sculpture*, exhibition catalogue, ed. Elisabeth L. Cameron (Los Angeles: UCLA Fowler Museum of Cultural History, 1996) 43–57.

16 Ibid., 43.

17 Collected and translated by Lawal 1996 (above n. 12) 129.

18 Pemberton 1982 (above n. 9) 138.

19 Idowu, 1962; cited in Lawal 1996 (above n. 12) 252.

20 Lawal 1996 (above n. 12) 253; Lawal (forthcoming).

21 Lawal 1996 (above n. 12) 121.

22 Henry John Drewal, "Gelede Masquerade: Imagery and Motif," *African Arts* 7.4 (1974) 8–19, 62–63.

23 Quoted in Joseph Nevadomsky, "The Benin Bronze Horseman as the Ata of Idah," *African Arts* 19.4 (1986) 40–47, and Barbara Blackmun, "Who Commissioned the Queen Mother Tusks? A Problem in the Chronology of Benin Ivories," *African Arts* 24.2 (1991) 54–65, 90.

24 Blackmun 1991 (above n. 23) 59–60.

25 Henry John Drewal and Margaret Drewal, "Projections from the Top in Yoruba Art," *African Arts* 11.1 (1977) 43–49.

26 Nevadomsky 1986 (above n. 23) 44.

27 Quoted in Rowland Abiodun, Henry John Drewal, and John Pemberton III, *Yoruba: Art and Aesthetics,* ed. Lorenz Homberger (New York and Zurich: The Center for African Art and the Rietberg Museum, 1991) 13.

28 Babatunde Lawal, personal communication, 1998.

29 Rowland Abiodun, "The Kingdom of Owo," in Drewal, Pemberton, and Abiodun 1989 (above n. 3) 93–96.

30 An early field photograph shows seven or eight very similar ivory figures belonging to the Benin Oromila priest, half of which are in pure Benin style, while the other half are—like this one—in the more imaginative style of Owo. William Fagg, personal communication to The Toledo Museum of Art, August 24, 1976.

31 Babatunde Lawal, personal communication, 1998.

32 Abiodun 1989 (above n. 29) 111.

33 Quoted in Frederick Lamp, "Frogs into Princes: The Temne Räbai Initiation," *African Arts* 11.2 (1978) 38–49, 94.

34 Ibid., 38.

35 Ibid.

36 W. A. Hart, "Masks with Metal-Strip Ornament from Sierra Leone," *African Arts* 20.3 (1987) 68–74, 90.

37 Quoted in Jan Vansina, "The Kuba Kingdom (Zaire)," in *Kings of Africa*, eds. Erna Beumers and Hans-Joachim Koloss (Maastricht: Foundation Kings of Africa, 1992) 73.

38 Joseph Cornet, "Masks among the Kuba Peoples," in *Face of the Spirits: Masks from the Zaire Basin*, eds. Frank Herreman and Constantijn Petridis (Ghent: Snoeck-Ducaju & Zoon, 1993) 129–36.

39 Ibid., 136.

40 Allen F. Roberts, "Insight, or Not Seeing is Believing," in Mary H. Nooter, *Secrecy: African Art That Conceals and Reveals* (New York and Munich: The Museum for African Art and Munich, 1993) 65.

41 Tamara Northern, *Art of Cameroon*, exhibition catalogue (Washington, D.C.: Smithsonian Institution Traveling Exhibition Service [SITES], 1984) 62.

42 After Patrick McNaughton, "Secret Sculptures of the Komo: Art and Power in Bamana Initiation Associations," in *Working Papers in the Traditional Arts* 4 (Philadelphia: Institute for the Study of Human Issues, 1979).

43 Nooter 1993 (above n. 40).

44 Tamara Northern, "Janus-Faced Crest Mask," in *African Art: The Barbier-Mueller Collection*, ed. Werner Schmalenbach (Munich: Prestel, 1988) 185.

45 Sarah Catherine Brett-Smith, "Speech Made Visible: The Irregular as a System of Meaning," in *Empirical Studies of the Arts* 2.2 (1984) 127–47.

46 Ibid., 146.

47 Ibid., 128.

48 Victoria Rovine, personal communication, 1998.

49 Patrick McNaughton, "The Shirts that Mande Hunters Wear," *African Arts* 15.3 (1982) 54–58, 91.

50 Sarah Catherine Brett-Smith, "Cloth as Amulet: The Anomalous Style of Basiae Mud Cloths,"

paper presented at the 11th Triennial Symposium on African Art, New Orleans, on the panel "Written Culture: Script and Inscription in Arts of Africa," chaired by Mary Nooter Roberts, April 10, 1998.

51 Brett-Smith 1984 (above n. 45) 142.

52 Eberhard Fischer and Lorenz Homberger, *Masks in Guro Culture, Ivory Coast*, exhibition catalogue (New York and Zurich: The Center for African Art and the Museum Rietberg, 1986), cited p. 16.

53 Ibid.

54 Lorenz Homberger, personal communication, 1998.

55 Susan Vogel, *Baule: African Art Western Eyes*, exhibition catalogue (New Haven and London: Yale University Press in association with The Museum for African Art, 1997) 138.

56 Ibid., 140.

57 Susan Vogel, personal communication, 1998.

58 Quoted in Vogel 1997 (above n. 55) 138.

59 Ibid., 196.

60 Ibid., 195–96, and personal communication, 1998.

61 Vogel 1997 (above n. 55) 199–202.

62 Brigitte Menzel, *Goldgewichte aus Ghana*, exhibition catalogue (Museum für Volkerkunde, Berlin, Neuefolge 12, *Abteilung Africa* III, 1968) 202–203.

63 Raymond A. Silverman, "Akan Kuduo: Form and Function," in *Akan Transformation: Problems in Ghanaian Art History*, eds. Doran H. Ross and Rioth F. Garrard (Los Angeles: UCLA Museum of Cultural History, Monograph Series 21, 1983) 11–12.

64 Ibid.

65 Doran H. Ross, personal communication, 1998.

66 Recorded by Emile Torday in the early

twentieth century and cited in David Binkley, "Cephalomorphic Palm Wine Cups," in *Treasures from the Africa-Museum, Tervuren*, exhibition catalogue (Tervuren: Royal Museum for Central Africa, 1995) 342–43.

67 Ibid., 342.

68 Ibid.

69 After Pemberton 1982 (above n. 9)162.

70 Herbert M. Cole, "Riders of Power: The Mounted Leader," in *Icons: Ideals and Power in the Art of Africa*, exhibition catalogue (Washington, D.C., and London: Smithsonian Institution Press, 1989) 116–35.

71 John Pemberton III, "The Oyo Empire," in Drewal, Pemberton, and Abiodun 1989 (above n. 3) 158–59.

72 Babatunde Lawal, personal communication, 1998.

73 Drewal, Pemberton, and Abiodun 1989 (above n. 3) 33.

74 Babatunde Lawal, personal communication, 1998.

75 Drewal, Pemberton, and Abiodun 1989 (above n. 3) 33.

76 Douglas Fraser and Herbert M. Cole, *African Art and Leadership* (Madison: University of Wisconsin Press, 1972) 326; also cited in Nancy Ingram Nooter, "East African High-Backed Stools: A Transcultural Tradition," *Tribal Arts* 2.3 (1995) 46.

77 Nooter 1995 (above n. 76) 46–60.

78 Allen F. Roberts, "Nyamwezi figure," in *Art and Life in Africa*, exhibition catalogue, ed. Christopher D. Roy (Seattle: The University of Washington Press for The University of Iowa Museum of Art, 1992) 248–49.

79 Allen F. Roberts, personal communication, 1998.

80 Nancy Ingram Nooter, personal communication, 1998.

81 Allen F. Roberts, "The Social and Historical Contexts of Tabwa Art," in *The Rising of a New Moon: A Century of Tabwa Art,* exhibition catalogue (Seattle: University of Washington Press for the University of Michigan Museum of Art, Ann Arbor, 1985).

82 Nooter 1995 (above n. 76) 46–60.

83 Cited p. 27 in Monni Adams, "Kuba Embroidered Cloth," *African Arts* 12.1 (1978) 24–39, 106.

84 Ibid., 30.

85 Ibid., 34.

86 Monni Adams, "Beyond Symmetry in Middle African Design," *African Arts* 22.1 (1981) 34–43, 102.

87 Robert Farris Thompson, *African Art in Motion* (Los Angeles: University of California Press, 1974) 10–11 and Adams 1981 (above n. 86).

88 Cited p. 23 in Eberhard Fischer, "Dan Forest Spirits: Masks in Dan Villages," *African Arts* 11.2 (1978) 16–23, 94.

89 Ibid., 23.

90 Ibid., 18.

91 Ibid., 19.

92 Ibid., 22–23.

93 Anita Glaze, *Art and Death in a Senufo Village* (Bloomington: Indiana University Press, 1981) 158.

94 Anita Glaze, personal communication, 1998.

95 Ibid.

96 Ibid.

97 Ibid.

98 Quoted p. 62 in Wyatt MacGaffey, "The Eyes of Understanding: Kongo Minkisi," in *Astonishment and Power,* exhibition catalogue (Washington, D.C.: Smithsonian Institution Press, 1993) 21–103.

99 Dunja Hersak, *Songye: Masks and Figure Sculpture* (London: Ethnographica, 1985) 118–22).

100 MacGaffey 1993 (above n. 98).

101 Dunja Hersak, "Nkishi statues," in *Masterpieces from Central Africa: The Tervuren Museum,* exhibition catalogue (New York and Munich: Prestel, 1996) 174–75.

102 Allen F. Roberts, *Animals in African Art: From the Familiar to the Marvelous,* exhibition catalogue (New York and Munich: The Museum for African Art and Prestel, 1995).

103 Roberts and Roberts 1996 (above n. 2) 204.

104 Michael Harris, "Resonance, Transformation, and Rhyme: The Art of Renée Stout," in *Astonishment and Power* (above n. 98) 107–53.

105 Quoted p. 277 in David Binkley, "The Teeth of Nyim: The Elephant and Ivory in Kuba Art," in *Elephant: The Animal and its Ivory in African Culture,* ed. Doran H. Ross, exhibition catalogue (Los Angeles: Fowler Museum of Cultural History, 1992) 277–91.

106 Ibid.

107 Ibid.

108 Jan Vansina, quoted in Adams 1978 (above n. 83) 27, 30.

109 Binkley 1992 (above n. 105) 286–88.

110 Louis Perrois, *Arts du Gabon: Les Arts Plastiques du Bassin de l'Ogooué* (Arnouville: Arts d'Afrique Noire and Paris: O.R.S.T.O.M., 1979).

111 Ibid., 100.

112 William Rubin, *'Primitivism' in 20th Century Art: Affinity of the Tribal and the Modern,* vol. 1 (New York: The Museum of Modern Art, 1984) 12–13.

113 T. Theuws, "Le Styx ambigu," *Bulletin du Centre d'études des problèmes sociaux indigènes* 81 (1968) 11.

114 Allen F. Roberts, *Threshold: African Art on the Verge* (forthcoming).

115 Leon Siroto, "The Face of the Bwiti," *African Arts* 1.1 (1968) 22–27, 86–89, 96.

116 Alain Chaffin and François Chaffin, *L'Art Kota: Les figures de reliquaires* (Meudon, 1979).

117 Alisa LaGamma, personal communication, 1998.

118 Siroto 1968 (above n. 115) 88.

119 E. E. Evans-Pritchard, "The Dance," in *Africa* 1.4 (1928) 447, cited in Enid Schildkrout and Curtis A. Keim, *African Reflections: Art from Northeastern Zaire,* exhibition catalogue (Seattle and London: University of Washington Press, in association with the American Museum of Natural History, New York, 1990) 211.

120 James Clifford, *Writing Culture: The Poetics and Politics of Ethnography,* ed. J. Clifford and G. E. Marcus (School of American Research Advanced Seminar; Berkeley, Los Angeles, London: University of California Press, 1990).

121 Roland Barthes, "The Face of Garbo," in *A Barthes Reader* (New York: Hill and Wang, The Noonday Press, 1982) 74.

122 Susan Stewart, *On Longing: Narratives of the Miniature, the Gigantic, the Souvenir, the Collection* (Durham and London: Duke University Press, 1993) 127.

Index